Leader and Teacher
Moissaye J. Olgin
First Prism Key Press Edition 2012

Prism Key Press
New York, NY 10001
PrismKeyPress.com

ISBN-13: 978-1470127008

Leader and Teacher

Moissaye J. Olgin

CONTENTS

M. J. Olgin, 1878-1939 7

"He Wrote His Name in the Hearts of the Masses" 11

"A Great Symbol of a Great Movement".................................. 13

The Real World of Tomorrow... 15

Jewish Reconstruction on the Order of the Day........................ 19

The Anti-Red Hysteria in the Jewish Field............................ 23

How Not to Argue Against Anti-Semitism.............................. 27

The Pest.. 31

Jewish Youth Speaks 35

Gorky.. 39

The Soviet Union and National Liberation 43

M. J. Olgin, 1878-1939

BORN March 24, 1878, in a little village near Kiev, Russia, Moissaye J. Olgin received a traditional education in Hebrew, and, after a short period of self-study, he entered the University of Kiev in 1900. It was at Kiev University that he first became active in the underground revolutionary movement.

He studied at the University of Heidelberg from 1907 to 1910, after which he returned to Russia where he became a writer and editor of numerous revolutionary and labor publications.

This work soon won for him a warm spot in the hearts of the Jewish masses, who were the special targets and victims of the ruthless terror of the tsarist regime. In 1901 he was elected chairman of the Students Central Committee, and was at the same time a member of the Jewish revolutionary student group, called "Freiheit." The tsarist regime ordered his arrest in April of 1903 on a charge of organizing Jewish self-defense groups against anticipated pogroms.

A year later Olgin left the university and went to Vilno as a member of the Vilno Committee of the Jewish Bund. A short while thereafter he was arrested but released on bail, whereupon he became a member of the editorial board of the Arbeiter Stimme (Labor's Voice).

He was the author of all the proclamations issued by the Central Committee of the Bund during the Revolution of 1905 while at the same time he prepared literary compositions for the illegal Jewish press.

His energy was inexhaustible. While editing newspapers and working with the underground organizations he also wrote books, short stories and numerous literary essays.

The first imperialist World War found him in Germany. Unable to return to Russia, Olgin came to the United States in 1915. Here he was very cordially welcomed by Jewish workers and intellectuals, among whom his writings were already popular. Soon after his arrival in the United States, he became a regular contributor to the Jewish daily Forward. Mastering the English language in an amazingly short time, by 1917 The Soul of the Russian Revolution, one of his outstanding books, was published.

In the meantime, he had continued his studies at Columbia University, and in 1918 received his Ph.D. degree. He lectured at the New School for Social Research in 1919.

Olgin was one of the founders of the Workers (Communist) Party in 1922. When the Jewish Socialist Federation split in 1921, Olgin severed his connections with the Forward. Later when the Federation united with the Communists, he was made one of the organizers of the Jewish section of the Party. He was a member of the National Committee of the Communist Party for many years.

Olgin was one of the founders of the Yiddish Daily Freiheit (now Morning Freiheit) and served as its editor up to the time of his death.

In 1937 Olgin went to Paris as delegation to the International Yiddish Culture Congress which founded the World Alliance for Jewish Culture (Y.C.U.F.). While in Paris he addressed the Writers Congress. Every year he toured the country lecturing on labor, social and cultural problems. He also made several trips to the Soviet Union.

Olgin was the author of a score of books and pamphlets. He was a magnificent linguist, a master of at least half a dozen languages: English, Russian, German, French, Polish, Hebrew and Yiddish. He wrote verse, essays, literary criticism and sociological studies. He would, with equal one of the American

8

effectiveness, write The Soul of the Russian Revolution and A Guide to Russian Literature and compose a pamphlet, Why Communism? which achieved a sale of nearly half a million in several languages.

He translated several volumes of Lenin's Collected Works from Russian into English; Frederick Engels' The Peasant War in Germany from German into Yiddish; John Reed's Ten Days That Shook the World from English into Yiddish; a volume of short stories from Polish into Yiddish; two volumes of tales of Mendele Moischer Sforim, the father of Jewish literature, from Hebrew into Yiddish; and Jack London's Call of the Wild from English into Yiddish.

At his funeral, on November 26, 1939, more than 100,000 workers took part in the procession, or lined the streets to pay tribute to a beloved leader.

"He Wrote His Name in the Heart of the Masses"

Statement of the National Committee of the Communist Party of the United States of America

The National Committee of the Communist Party of the United States records with the deepest sorrow the death of Moissaye J. Olgin on the morning of November 22, 1939. Comrade Olgin was the outstanding and most beloved figure in the Jewish community, whose influence extended far beyond the borders of America, as well as a leading member of the Communist Party since 1922. As the editor of the Morning Freiheit since its foundation, he was mainly responsible for its growing influence, and for the high literary quality which characterized its pages, reflecting his wide culture and his own distinguished talents as an artist, which attracted many worthy collaborators. Unexcelled as an orator, Comrade Olgin wore himself out meeting the demands upon his services as a speaker, among the broadest masses as well as directly for the Party, whose candidate he was in many election campaigns in New York.

After almost two years' illness, during which Comrade Olgin continued from his sickbed a prolific literary work for the Freiheit, for the Daily Worker, and as special correspondent of Pravda, Moscow, he had apparently improved in health so greatly that he appeared in Madison Square garden, on November 13, for his first public speech since he was stricken. No one present at that meeting can forget the demonstration Comrade Olgin received on that occasion, which fittingly registered the deep mass affection for him that lives in the hearts of the workers; fruit of his long years of selfless devotion to their interests. The 22,000 workers in that audience did not realize that they were exchanging the final greetings with one of the most outstanding of their representatives, on behalf of the hundreds of thousands, yes millions, who will mourn the great loss we have all suffered at his death.

Comrade Olgin would have asked no better setting for his last days than his active service in the cause of the working class, of socialism, of the Communist Party, which he carried on to his last hours, in which he found the fullest realization of his life-long aspirations.

Moissaye J. Olgin wrote his name indelibly in the hearts of the masses whom he served. The National Committee of the CPUSA joins with these masses in their sorrow, and calls upon all who felt Olgin's inspiring influence to close their ranks, with the same enthusiasm he showed, for victory in the battles name beginning.

William Z. Foster, Chairman

Earl Browder, General Secretary

"A Great Symbol of a Great Movement"

Speech delivered by the General Secretary of the Communist Party, U. S. A., at the funeral of Moissaye J. Olgin, at the Royal Windsor, New York, November 26, 1939.

IT IS A difficult and painful thing to say our farewells to a great friend, comrade, fellow-fighter, and fellow worker, who has become so intimately a part of the life of our great movement that it is difficult to think of his being gone from us.

Comrade Olgin, by a long life of struggle and of service to the masses, has become much more than an individual; he became a great symbol of a great movement. Comrade Olgin's life and work, expressing that movement, carrying it to higher and higher stages, became great with the movement which he served. At all the great turning points, Comrade Olgin found his way with unerring instinct, that same instinct which always kept him in the closest bonds with the broad masses of the workers; and Comrade Olgin helped thousands and tens of thousands to find the correct path in this struggle.

I think that Comrade Olgin would not have wished to leave us. He was a man who loved life, a man greedy for every morsel of life, greedy for life for the masses, for the people and jealous of everything that reduced or attacked the possibilities of life for the masses.

Especially Comrade Olgin would have wanted to be with us through the great battles now beginning — but if he knew that the parting had to be now I am sure Comrade Olgin would have wanted it to be as it was — that he passed as a warrior, in battle, to the last moment engaged in the fight against the enemies of the people, to the last moment flinging scorn upon them, the traitors, the weak of heart, those who

13

flinched and turned away from the battle; to the last moment he was the great tribune of the people, to the last moment he was performing the true function of the Bolshevik, of the Communist, of the one who finds life rich and well worth living because it is at the service of the Party of the working class and of the people, in which service the life laid down becomes ever more significant and worthwhile.

In the life and in the death of Comrade Olgin we have the example of that which makes our class the representative of the future of humanity itself, which makes our class the protector and the bearer of human culture for future history, of that which makes of all parties, the Communist Party vanguard of human progress, the guarantee that the forces of darkness will not prevail.

Comrade Olgin stands for all these things to each and every one of us. Comrade Olgin lives in the heart and memory of this movement. Comrade Olgin's contribution is imperishable.

And so we say farewell to our great friend, to our great comrade and fellow-fighter. From his life, his work, from his death we gather new strength, new determination, new enthusiasm to march forward to the defeat of all the enemies of mankind; to the defeat of imperialism that threatens to destroy the world today; to the defeat of capitalist exploitation; to the defeat of race hatreds and intolerance and everything that divides man from man; to the defeat of all class and national oppression and exploitation; to the victory of the working class, to the victory of the people, to the victory of socialism — this is what Comrade Olgin means to us, and this day is a day not only of sorrowful parting but a day of firm and vigorous advance to the realization of the great cause for which Comrade Olgin was head and body.

The Real World Of Tomorrow

HERE is a shelf in the Hall of Science, Literature and the Press in the Soviet Pavilion at the World's Fair. On this shelf there are specimens of books produced in the Soviet Union. As I handled these books one after the other to learn the name of the authors, to scrutinize the paper, the printing and the binding — which, by the way, are excellent — I discovered also a book in Yiddish. It was a volume of folk songs with notes. The book is printed on fine paper with an artistic finish, and the binding is soft leather which it is a joy to touch. The book would be a grand addition to the library of the most fastidious book-collector. It looks like a true work of love: both the text, carefully chosen and arranged, and the exterior bespeak an attitude of great respect and affection for the work at hand.

I held this book in my hands and I thought that this is perhaps the only Yiddish book in the entire Fair. There isn't a single pavilion of any other nation where Yiddish books are shown. There isn't a single nation in the world which has that attitude of deference and fondness for the cultures of minority nationalities which we find in the Soviet Union. On that shelf the Jewish book is not the only representative of a cultural minority; there are books in Georgian, in Armenian, in Uzbek, in Tartar, not to speak of the books in the Ukrainian language which was persecuted and suppressed before 1917.

When you walk through the Hall of Art of the Soviet Pavilion, you will see paintings, sculptures, wood-carvings, embroideries, lacquered woodwork produced by the various Soviet peoples. The work of each one is cherished, collected, shown to the world.

After leaving the Soviet Pavilion, I read in a paper on the train the Nth declaration that the Soviet Union gives no

15

freedom to its citizens and that the Soviet Union is classed with Germany and Italy among the totalitarian states. I do not know whether to laugh in derision or cry in anger. On second thought I remain calm. The truth cannot be concealed, I say to myself. The truth, like life, has its own irresistible power. In our days you cannot keep it away from the people for long.

* * *

In one of the latest issues of the Yiddish magazine Shtern published in Minsk, there is a facsimile of an official letter addressed by the governor of Minsk to the chief of police of Minsk, dated 1914. The letters reads as follows:

"To the Minsk Chief of Police:

"I instruct your High Nobility to inform Boruch, Davidov Krasner, who resides in the city of Minsk, in Zacharyevsky Alley, in the house of Shapiro; that his petition about permission to arrange a reading by the writer-humorist Sholom Aleichem (Sch. Rabinovich) in the spoken Jewish language in the town of Baranovichi, has been left by me without satisfying it.

"You are to collect from the said person stamp tax in this case to the amount of 1 ruble and 50 kopeks and to deposit that sum in the local treasury as income of the treasury department, and to inform the Minsk treasury chamber about it."

In 1914 one needed the governor's permission to organize a reading by Sholom Aleichem of his work. In most cases this was prohibited. From the same magazine it is evident that another reading which a society wished to organize for Sholom Aleichem in Minsk also failed to obtain the governor's permission.

This year the Soviet Union is celebrating the eightieth birthday of Sholom Aleichem. It is a celebration not only of the Jews but of the entire Soviet Union. Many of the wonderful stories and sketches by Sholom Aleichem have been translated into Russian and a variety of other languages. Sholom Aleichem's works are being distributed in hundreds of thousands of copies....

Jewish Reconstruction on the Order of the Day

Two million Jews have been taken over by the Soviet Union. The territory of Western Ukraine and Western Byelo-Russia that will now join the Ukrainian Soviet Socialist Republic and the Byelo-Russian Soviet Socialist republic, is a little less than one-half of the former territory of the Polish state, which contained 3,500,000 Jews. It is now admitted that the number of Jews residing in the territories that have just passed under the Hammer and Sickle is about two million.

This is the Soviet contribution to the solution of the Jewish refugee problem. For years the Jewish reactionaries kept on baiting the Communists here on the role of the Soviet Union in caring for refugees. Because the Soviet government made no noise about the admittance of refugees into its land, the reactionaries concluded that the USSR cared little for the fate of those who ran away from the fascist hangmen. Even then, the number of refugees finding their way into the Soviet union was large. But now the Soviet Union has taken over two million Jews who only three months ago would have been happy to run away from the Polish pogrom-rule. The Soviet Union has become a grand asylum for two million of the most persecuted, most harassed, frequently murdered, at all times degraded Jewish people.

When one speaks of an asylum one pictures a place of refuge where the refugee is left to shift for himself. At best a refugee in the capitalist countries is given some aid from charitable institutions and, since he is allowed to live in the country, he is expected to ask no more.

The Jews of Western Ukraine and Western Byelo-Russia, with the incorporation of these territories into the

USSR, become citizens of the Union and of the respective Republics. They are not "aliens." They are not "guests." They are not there on sufferance. They are full-fledged citizens of a mighty land, and they are granted all rights, privileges, and opportunities for a new life.

* * * * *

Yet the problem of establishing the new life of the two million Jews on a firm foundation economically will require a great amount of constructive work. The possibilities for solving the economic problem are there in great abundance. The Soviet Union needs the skill, the brains, the creativeness of millions and millions. Yet the skill and creativeness will — in many cases& #8212; first have to be developed.

The overwhelming majority of those two million are toilers: shop workers, artisans, petty traders, white collar workers and a host of those engaged in all kinds of non-descript occupations which breed among the Jewish people when they are cut off from the main economic basis of the country. Briefly, the composition of the Jewish people in Western Ukraine and Western Byelo-Russia is about the same as was the composition of the Jewish people under the tsar: few workers of large industrial establishments — since Jews were simply excluded from major factories and plants. Many workers employed in smaller factories and shops, some of them only three or four workers. Many "independent" artisans who, starving themselves, kept one or two journeymen and apprentices on a below-starvation level. A tremendous number of people engaged in midget trade, working day and night, and unable to eke out a meager living. A host of so-called "Luftmenschen" having no visible source of livelihood, reaching out for every chance occupation, actually starving, living partly on charity, partly on donations from abroad. An ungodly number of paupers, beggars, wanderers, homeless. . . . The Polish state made a conscious effort to shut the Jews off from the national

20

economy. The Polish state officially declared that there were one million Jews "too many" in the country.

* * * * *

All the Jews not now engaged in productive work will have to be reconstructed. For this, too, there are precedents. The Soviet government reconstructed great masses of the Jews taken over from tsarism. The work was done along many lines. Jewish workers are admitted into all industrial establishments. Jewish workers are encouraged to improve their qualifications in order to be able to enter the best plants. Jewish artisans were encouraged to form cooperative producing organizations using raw materials supplied by the government and selling their products to state and cooperative organizations. Those who knew no trade at all were taught a trade. Cultural workers were given opportunity to improve their knowledge and to become useful in all kinds of Soviet institutions like schools, libraries, etc. white collar workers were given jobs. All of them were organized in trade unions and in other organizations and the level of their education raised. Those fit and willing to do agricultural work were given land and aided in settling as collective farmers.

All this will have to be done now among the two million Jews. Under these conditions the Jewish autonomous region, Bir-Bidjan, with its vast potentialities acquires greater significance. It is there where hundreds of thousands of new Jews can go in the very near future to start a new life in their own country.

The important thing is that the initial settling of the new virgin land has already been done. The work of the new settlers will be incomparably more easy.

The Anti-Red Hysteria in the Jewish Field

As soon as the non-aggression pact between the Soviet Union and Germany was announced, a number of Jewish liberals reacted by coming out violently against the Soviet Union and against the Communists in the United States.

The reason advanced was that the pact endangered the lives of the Jews of Europe. So it was clearly stated, for instance, in a declaration of several Jewish writers explaining why they had quit the non-partisan Y.C.U.F. (World Alliance for Jewish Culture). The Stalin-Hitler alliance, they said, was placing the 3,500,000 Jews of Poland in danger of death. The writers did not hesitate to call the pact an "alliance." They were certain that the Soviet Union had promised Hitler military aid. They were certain that, outside the clauses of the non-aggression pact as announced, there were also secret clauses that spelled the strengthening of the Nazis and the ruin of the Jews.

Events have proved that these writers and those who thought in the same vein were wrong. There is no military alliance between the USSR and Germany. There is no collaboration in any respect between the USSR and Germany except that which is natural when two states are on a footing of non-aggression. The Soviet Union is trading with Germany but it is also trading with England. The Soviet Union is insisting on a speedy termination of the war and it will certainly insist on a just peace in the interests of the peoples of all countries.

Of the greatest immediate importance for the Jews is the fact that the Soviet Union, basing itself on the non-aggression pact and utilizing the situation when Western Ukraine and Western Byelo-Russia remained no-man's land after the collapse of the Polish government, marched into those territories and liberated from the yoke of fascism 13,000,000 people, among them two million Jews.

This introduced a radical change in the status of the Jews of Europe. It will have far-reaching consequences which cannot even be fully predicted today. For one thing, the number of the Jews in the USSR has increased from three million to five million, which means that the specific weight of the Jewish population in the USSR has become greater. Cultural activities among the Jews of the USSR will increase accordingly. Five million Jews under the free Soviet regime are something which only two short months ago one could not dream.

The prospect is that, horrible as is the situation of the Jews in Central Europe, a change to the better is imminent. In the Baltic states the change is taking place now. The Jews in Poland and in Germany will see a new day with the establishment of a European peace. That peace cannot be established without the cooperation of the Soviet Union. And where such a cooperation exists, there the rights of the small nations will be made a major issue.

That being the case, one would expect that some of the liberal Jews who foresaw dire consequences for the Jews from the non-aggression pact would change their stand. Unfortunately, this has not yet taken place. It is possible that some revision of opinions is going on among a few of the Jewish liberals. But it has not yet come into the open by way of public expression.

* * * * *

We are living in an atmosphere of anti-Red hysteria among the Jews. It so happens that three out of the four metropolitan Yiddish papers are playing a disproportionately large role in the public life of the Jews. From everyday experience we know that the Jewish population, organized and unorganized, is not in accord with those three papers. Yet it is

24

they that seem to give the tone to Jewish public life. It is their opinions that pass as Jewish public opinion generally. And they keep on abusing the Soviet Union, slandering its leadership, distorting every bit of information about Soviet activities, concealing from the masses the significance of the liberation of two million Jews, picturing it as an event fraught with danger if not as a calamity, denouncing everyone who happens to agree with the peace policy of the Soviet Union, and conducting a red-baiting campaign of the most vociferous and unscrupulous kind.

Why is it so? What is back of this barrage? Is it conviction? There can be no question of adhering to honest convictions where falsification and distortion are the order of the day. Out paper has its hands full catching the journalists of these three papers red-handed. No words are strong enough to brand the ugly manipulations of these journalists, who keep mum about highly important events, present rumors as fact, and parade invention as news.

Do these people not realize that they are treading on dangerous ground? Why is it that this Red-baiting campaign is going one? Do they not understand that by doing the work of the worst reactionaries in the United States they are endangering civil liberties, and thereby the status of the Jews?

How Not To Argue Against Anti-Semitism

WHEN you argue against anti-Semitism, do not put yourself on the anti-Semite's level. Do not take his premises for granted. Do not wish to set him straight "from his own point of view." Rather put yourself on the general basis of democracy which the overwhelming majority of the people accept. Argue from the point of view of general decency and good-neighborliness. Above all things expose the social forces behind anti-Semitism, explain which group tries to benefit by anti-Semitism. In doing so you will raise the level of political and social understanding of the people you address yourself to, and in this way combat anti-Semitism.

The authors of the pamphlet, Father Coughlin, His 'Facts' and Arguments,[1] have devoted nearly one-half of their work to proving that Jewish bankers of the United States did not finance the Bolshevik Revolution. This was a good piece of work; in fact too good, for it produced too formidable an array of facts to disprove an obviously silly statement. But in doing so the authors, unfortunately, placed the argument on the basis of Coughlin's "Weltanschauung." They assumed together with Coughlin that Communism is bad, that Communism must be fought. The second half of their pamphlet is devoted to proving that Communism has brought the Jews nothing but sufferings and persecution. One of their chapters is entitled, "How Jews Have Been Persecuted Under Communism." They quote a statement that "thinking Jews the world over see the liquidation of the Communist regime in Russia as the only salvation for their co-religionists in that unhappy land." They quote another statement that "two and a half million men and women are placed between an appalling present and an even more appalling future, placed by the choice between a Red and White dictatorship, between dying out and dying a violent death." The readers are not only deprived of the information that the Soviet Union is the only country in which there is practically no anti-Semitism and in which Jewish life is flourishing on the basis of equality and freedom, but they are given the false information that Jews are dying out in the Soviet Union.

* * * * *

What is wrong with this line of argument? It is placed on a Red-baiting and not on a democratic foundation.

An adherent of democracy, in arguing against anti-Semitism, should point out that the principle of democracy implies equality of all nationalities, whether the individual citizen likes individuals of other nationalities or the doings of certain groups among them or not. The principle of democracy takes it for granted that any nationality or "race" is entitled to have its own bankers, clergy, manufacturers, workers, reactionaries, Communists. The principle of democracy forbids blaming a whole nationality for the doings of some of its members or to blame one single nationality for the evils of the whole world. The principle of democracy demands that all the oppressed of all nationalities should unite against their oppressors.

Another basic element in an argument against anti-Semitism is the explanation of the purpose for which anti-Semitism is being fostered.

* * * * *

In the present case it is possible to expose Coughlin, showing his connection with the open shop employers, with the attacks on unemployment relief. In other words, Coughlin's anti-Semitism must be exposed as a link in the chain of reaction with which the economic royalists wish to strangle the people of the United States. No argument against anti-Semitism will be convincing enough unless it shows that anti-Semitism tends to spread mistrust between Jewish workers and non-Jewish workers to the benefit of the open shop manufacturers and to the detriment of the labor movement which is the bulwark of democracy in our country. He who argues against anti-Semitism must show that the spread of anti-Semitism is in the interests of those who would lower the standards of living of the people and make them pay the bill for economic crisis — which is exactly what fascism is forcing the people to suffer in totalitarian states.

All this is missing in the General Jewish Council's pamphlet. The non-Jew who will read that pamphlet will not learn either the nature of anti-Semitism or the means to combat it. He may learn that on certain occasions Coughlin made incorrect statements, but he will also learn to hate and despise the only country in the world in which the Jews are perfectly free and in which anti-Semitism is a curse of the past.

There are some Jews who think that you can approach a non-Jew with your propaganda against anti-Semitism while leaving him a prey to other prejudices. This line of thought even assumes that one may agree with a Dies, a Hague or a Harvey, if only one shows them that anti-Semitism is wrong. In reality you cannot show that anti-Semitism is wrong unless you show that reaction is wrong and that fascism is a menace.

And this is exactly where the present pamphlet falls flat.

Notes

1. Issued by the General Jewish Council.

The Pest

You can find him everywhere, in editorial rooms, in business offices, in schools, in any other place where you may happen to start a casual conversation. He is displeased, to say the least. Everything is going to the dogs, he says. Everything is just growing worse and worse. The situation of the Jews? Horrible. Haven't you heard what the Nazis are doing in Prague? Business? Why, making a living is becoming more difficult with every month, and if anybody promises you an improvement he just doesn't know what he is talking about. America? This country is certainly doomed to fall prey to fascism; all indications are to this effect.

Before you know it, the man is pouring forth a stream of complaints, and as you listen to him you feel that a dark cloud is enveloping you and making you choke.

This type is to be found among all strata of American society today, but it seems to me it is a special blessing of the Jewish people.

The trouble with these talkers is that they consider their talk a public service. They imagine they are politically minded. They think that what they sputter at every occasion is a much needed clarification of world events. Why, things are so bad in our days, fascism is on the march, the Jews are being oppressed more and more, anti-Semitism is growing in the United States, American democracy can easily be superseded by something like fascism, the world situation is rotten, business is on the decline, and so on and so forth. . . . After our complainer has been complaining for about five or ten or sixty minutes he thinks he has done something important for society. When you try to argue with him he proudly declares he cannot be convinced by "unfounded" assertions, that in our times one has to expect the worst.

* * * * *

Dear friends, when you meet a fellow like this, don't argue with him. Isolate him. Make him harmless. Treat him as a problem case, not as a normal human being who has to be persuaded. People of this type cannot be persuaded because in most cases they have no social outlook but only spleen.

Unfortunately such types are the affliction of our days. What socially-minded people have to do is to make it clear to anybody they meet that complaining is easy but fighting is much more difficult, that whining is the resort of the weak when resistance is called for, that drawing dark pictures is a destructive job at a time when a way out of difficulties is to be sought.

To counteract the degrading influence of the whiners we must always hold before our eyes that basic forces that make for progress and the ways in which these forces assert themselves. Sometimes it is necessary to go to fundamentals. The basic thing is that the people of the world, and in the first place the people of the United States, do not want either fascism or war. Public resentment against fascist and imperialist barbarities has been steadily mounting both in the democratic countries and in the countries dominated by the fascists. Public indignation against the torturing of the Jews grew to colossal proportions after Munich. In America, consciousness of the value of democratic institutions and fear of losing them has become widespread as never before. Mass insistence on the right of every man, woman and youth to a job, if not in private industry then on a government project, has become a growing feature of public sentiment in our country. Dislike of big business rule has become so widespread that even the worst reaction of the large capitalist combines disguises itself as "progressive" and caring for the interests of the people. The labor movement in this country is growing and adopting an ever more progressive

32

program. Socialist ideas, i.e., consciousness of the necessity of replacing capitalism by a socially-owned and operated economy, is now to be found among many millions of people who not long ago worshipped at the shrine of the capitalist system. The influence of the USSR as a country where socialism has become a fact and as a great power standing guard on the international frontiers to defend peace and encourage democracy has penetrated into large masses throughout the world.

As against the complainers you must make it clear that a program of action is imperative. He who is concerned with carrying out a program has no time to whine.

Jewish Youth Speaks

"Ah, what do I care about Yiddish! I am an American and that's enough for me!"

This is the typical attitude of a great many young Jewish men and women; this is their "confession of faith" when confronted with the problems of Jewish life and Jewish culture.

It is an incorrect attitude, It is an unhealthy confession. It ignores the facts.

Hardly anyone among the "I-don't-care" Jewish youth will dare say or think that Jewish life as such is no business of theirs at the present historical juncture. Jewish life is a momentous problem now not only for the Jews but for progressive mankind as a whole. Fascism is intent on destroying the Jewish people. Anti-Semitism, the sharp weapon of reaction and fascism, is out to make Jewish life a curse. Progressive mankind must resist. The Jews must resist.

Resistance to the enemy, counter-attack against anti-Semitism will be effective only when the Jewish people unite their forces. To unite forces the people must understand each other. They must have common ground. They must, at east, be on speaking grounds. And are they on speaking terms when so many Jewish youth declare: "I don't care about Yiddish"?

Yiddish, don't you see, happens to be a part of the life of the Jewish masses. It is their language. It is the instrument of their self-expression. It is the instrument of the culture of millions of Jews in this country and abroad, and the culture created in that language is equal to the cultures created in other languages. There is no way of separating the Jewish people from the Yiddish language. There is no way of separating culture in Yiddish from Jewish life.

A young Jewish man or woman wishing to function in the present historical era as part of the progressive forces against anti-Semitism and fascism cannot have the "I-don't-care" attitude towards the Yiddish language and culture, whether he or she speaks Yiddish or not.

There is another angle to the situation. The "I-don't-care" mentality is just what anti-Semitism endeavors to develop among the Jews. What can be better for anti-Semitism than indifference or disdain on the part of the younger Jews to what large masses of the Jewish people consider their cherished inheritance and precious possession?

*   *   *   *   *

It is with the desire to overcome this attitude that a conference of young Jewish men and women met recently under the auspices of the World Alliance for Jewish Culture (Y.C.U.F.), American Section. The conference adopted a declaration which says that "particularly alarming is the situation of Jewish youth in America, a large part of which is little connected with the life of the Jewish people and with Jewish culture." The conference declared that the assembled intended to help create a closer bond between Jewish youth and the Jewish people.

The Y.C.U.F. is not a political but a cultural organization. It looks upon progressive secular culture as the platform on which most of the Jewish forces can unite. It proceeds from the correct assumption that a cultural unification of the Jewish people will make them stronger and more capable to resist attacks from without and from within. The Youth group organized at the conference makes it its aim to help heal the breach between the younger and the older generations. Their program calls for work both among the Yiddish-speaking and among the English-speaking youth...

The newly created Youth Group deserves the greatest

attention of progressive Jewish youth.

Gorky
Born March 28, 1868; died June 18, 1936

BARELY five years ago I heard Gorky addressing the All-Union Congress of Soviet Writers. He was dean of Soviet letters in more than one sense. He had written numerous novels, stories, sketches and plays that occupied first place in world literature as works of art. He had inaugurated and helped develop the literature of the workers, proletarian literature springing from the factories and shops. He had guided the talent of numerous young writers who found in him a teacher, a counsellor, an inspirer. He had written great, eloquent tracts against world reaction and fascism that made a profound impression not only in the Soviet Union, but in many other countries. He had initiated and encouraged the publication of collective works springing from the very depth of the working people, among them the now famous History of the Factories and Plants in which the workers themselves became historians of a past so close to their heart. He had been the editor of almanacs and series of novels and other publications. He had written scores and scores of letters of advice to collective farms and youth organizations, to Red Army units and labor unions, to writers' groups and village teachers. He had led a colorful and fruitful and profound life - as broad as the Revolution which changed as by magic one-sixth of the surface of the earth.

There he stood, a man rich with achievement beyond anything a writer could wish for himself. Yet he looked neither aged in spite of his sixty-six years, nor conscious of his greatness. He was just a man who had to carry through a piece of work. He was the chairman of that gathering of the best there was in the writing community of the U.S.S.R. He had to put that Congress on the level it deserved as the greatest convention of those whom Stalin called "the engineers of the human soul," whose work is of a nature that it molds the minds of scores of millions in a country where socialism is the order of the day.

He looked neither old nor tired in spite of a sickness that plagued him for the better part of forty years, nor "dictatorial," as some foreign enemies described him in their malice. He was a man of creative intelligence, a man of ideas, a man shot through with the passion of thinking that was called to change the face of life.

* * * * *

There was another side to that Congress, and to Gorky, which made the occasion particularly thrilling to me as a Jewish writer. The man Gorky had aided the development of the literatures of national minorities in old Russia: the Ukrainians, the Georgians, the White Russians, the Jews. After the Revolution he had devoted a large part of his activities to encouraging the growth of literatures other than Russian in the U.S.S.R. Standing on that platform of the All-Union Congress, at which were gathered not only the Russian writers but the writers of all the other republics and regions and languages in the country, he said:

"I find it necessary to point out that the Soviet literature is not only the literature of the Russian language; this is an all-Union literature. The literatures of the brother republics, being different from us in language only, live and work in the light and under the beneficent influence of the same idea."

* * * * *

Gorky had a great admiration for Jewish literature. In the magazine Screen for 1938, memoirs were printed about Gorky's relation to Jewish writers.

"Alexei Maximovich," says the author, "became extremely enthusiastic over Sholem Aleichem's story Chanukah

Gelt, the amazing humor of which was fully appreciated by Gorky. He very much liked the stories by Peretz. He once looked for a long while at a Peretz portrait brought to him, then he asked:

"'Why shouldn't he come here?'"

"I answered that Peretz could not do that.

"Gorky was astonished:

"'Why?'

"'He has no right to live outside of the Jewish pale of settlement.'

"Alexei Maximovich kept quiet for a while, pressing his lips sternly, then he said slowly and emphatically: "'Scoun-dr-els!'"

That was at the beginning of the twentieth century. Gorky was then busy organizing the publication of a volume of translations into Russian from Jewish authors. The volume was ready, but in the meantime Gorky was arrested and exiled. The volume never appeared. But Gorky's interest in Jewish literature never flagged.

* * * * *

In a letter to the Ukrainian writer Kotzyubinsky (1913), Gorky said: "A man is mortal, a people is immortal."

"A man is mortal, a people is immortal."

This great reverence for people, for the equality of people, for the culture of people, guided him till his very last.

He would have lived with us longer had he not been murdered by assassins, servants of fascism. Too dangerous was the man to his mortal enemy, fascism.

The Soviet Union and National Liberation

Speech delivered by M. J. Olgin before 22,000 in Madison Square Garden, New York, November 13, 1939, in celebration of the twenty-second anniversary of the Socialist Revolution

ON THIS twenty-second anniversary of the October Revolution we greet the people, the government, the leadership of that country in which exploitation of man by man is no more, and in which national oppression has been supplanted by unity and brotherly cooperation of scores of nationalities adhering to the principle that the well-being and the cultural growth of each is the guarantee of the happiness of all.

Well do I remember the time when tsarist Russia was "the prison of nations." Myself a member of one of the most oppressed and persecuted peoples of Russia, I witnessed ruthless suppression of Jews, Ukrainians, Byelo-Russians, Tartars, Turkmen, Georgians, Armenians and other nationalities who were not even accorded the name of "people" but were contemptuously labelled "inorodtsy" ("those differently born"). The inorodtsy were treated as colonial peoples within the Russian Empire: they were subjected to a more severe economic exploitation and they were deprived of political rights even more brutally than were the Great-Russian people; their languages and cultures were not recognized and the use of the mother tongue often punished.

The Social-Democrats, the Socialist-Revolutionaries spoke of "self-determination" of nationalities. But when the February Revolution of 1917 came and the Social-Democrats and Socialist-Revolutionaries gained power through the Kerensky government, they continued the oppression of over forty per cent of the populations of Russia — in the interests of the Russian capitalists and landlords. There was only one party which as early as April, 1917, framed a program, declaring the right of self-determination to mean real freedom for all nationalities, including the right to secede if its people wished to do so. That party was the Bolshevik Party under the leadership of Lenin. The revolutionist who framed the April thesis about national liberation was Joseph Stalin.

NATIONAL OPPRESSION BANISHED

When the Bolsheviks seized power in October, 1917, when the Soviets became the government of Russia, one of the first acts of the new regime was to establish full freedom, full equality for the numerous peoples within the frontiers of the Soviet state.

By this a new principle was introduced in the interrelation of peoples — the principle of peaceful and friendly co-existence and cooperation of various nationalities, not only not fighting each other, not only not oppressing each other, but on the contrary, aiding each other both culturally and economically. The Soviet Union has become a league of nations of its own. And while the League of Nations organized at Versailles suffered one ignominious defeat after the other, the family of nations established within the U.S.S.R. grew in strength, developed its members materially and spiritually and now holds out to the world an example of how it is possible to do away with national oppression, how it is possible to solve the national problem to the mutual benefit of all concerned.

This was possible only in consequence of the fact that economic exploitation was abolished by the October Revolution. Where there are no ruling classes there can be no ruling nations either. Where there is no capitalism there can be no imperialist tendencies, no desire for imperialist domination-

and no national oppression. Where the people, the toiling people, workers, farmers, intellectuals, are masters of their own destinies through a freely chosen government — as is the case in the Soviet Union — there the flourishing of the life of the toiling people is the major common aim, the raising of the economic status of everybody is the collective task, and this can be best achieved when the cultures of every nationality and the culture of every individual toiler within the nationality are developed, when every nationality is given the right to live its own cultural life.

THE DEVELOPMENT OF NATIONAL CULTURES

"A culture national in form and socialist in substance" is the program formulated for all the nationalities within the Soviet Union by the leader of nations, Stalin. A culture national in form and socialist in substance could develop most vigorously only where the material well being was improved. Under the leadership of the Communist Party of the Soviet Union and Comrade Stalin, the Russian nationality, being more advanced economically than many others within the framework of the U.S.S.R., has contributed of its financial and other resources to help the development of the formerly exploited and oppressed nationalities.

The new principle, the socialist principle in the interrelation between nationalities, is that of friendship instead of hatred, mutual aid instead of suppression, equality of all races instead of the division into "superior" and "inferior" races insidiously preached by spokesmen of imperialism and made into an official dogma by fascism.

The Jews were among the most oppressed in tsarist Russia. The Jews were practically removed from most of the sources of making a living. The Jews were treated like pariahs.

The Jews were subjected to pogroms. The Soviet government had to do a tremendous amount of reconstruction work in order to transform millions of Jews into productive elements of society. That work was accomplished with an immense amount of care and consideration. In order that the Jews may be able to develop statehood within the Soviet Union, a Jewish Autonomous Region was designated to them in one of the most fertile territories in the Far East. That region is known as Biro-Bidjan. In due time it will be transformed into the J.S.S.R. (Jewish Soviet Socialist Republic).

NATIONAL HATRED IS GONE

Every step of the Soviet Union was a hard blow at capitalism. The seizure of power over one-sixth of the surface of the earth was more than a slap. It eliminated capitalist rule, capitalist mismanagement, capitalist inefficiency, capitalist bloody brutality over one-sixth of the earth's surface. Every subsequent act was a new defeat for world capitalism.

Socialism is impossible, said the "best" minds among capitalist theoreticians. Socialism has been constructed and is a fact which even the blind must take notice of.

Industrial progress is impossible without the "master minds" of private owners, said the same and other theoreticians. The Communist Party of the Soviet Union, under the leadership of Comrade Stalin, has lifted Russia from the status of the most backward to that of the most advanced industrial country in Europe, second only to the United States of America.

Hate among nations is a principle of human nature, said bourgeois theoreticians. The Bolsheviks only laughed. The Bolsheviks said that human nature too could be changed, and they set out to change it. What seemed impossible in relation to

46

nationalities is now a fact. National hatreds are a thing of the dark past in the U.S.S.R. National hatreds cannot be even comprehended by the new Soviet generations. National cultures blossomed up in a manner unknown anywhere in the world.

Every step of the Soviet Union has been a challenge to imperialism. Every move of the socialist state has met with slander, abuse, intrigue and attempts at thwarting and weakening the challenger. Thus it has been during the twenty-two years of the existence of the U.S.S.R. Thus it is today. Out of the first World War emerged the Soviet Union. Out of the second World War there has emerged, so far, the establishment of Soviets in a territory inhabited by thirteen million formerly oppressed people.

"A BEACON FOR BLEEDING HUMANITY"

What new advances the Soviet principle will make in the course of the present war the coming months will show. The Sovietization of Western Ukraine and Western Byelo-Russia has thrown into the boldest relief the difference between capitalist rule and Soviet people's rule. There, oppression aggravated by war; here, liberation. There, the attempt to turn conquered nations into slaves; here, all resources of a powerful country set in motion to make the lives of the new citizens happier, to open before them the great opportunities that only a socialist system can offer. There, the lash, the bayonet, the concentration camp, the pogrom; here, a helping friendly hand, an upswing of cultural activities, encouragement to people to think, to develop, to govern themselves in their native tongue, to rise to the highest levels of art, science, education, creative thought.

Western Ukraine and Western Byelo-Russia stand in a clear socialist light as a beacon for bleeding humanity. This is the way out. This is she solution for the problems which capitalism can only sharpen but never solve.

When we see capitalist propagandists raging; when we hear Social-Democratic, Trotskyite, Lovestoneite lackeys of imperialism barking at the new active policy of the Soviet Union in world affairs; when we see the press unloosing a barrage of hostile comment against the Soviet Union, when we are surrounded by poison-pen and poison-mouth befoulers of the Soviet Union of the Dies-Coughlin-Waldman-Krivitsky and other stoolpigeon and provocateur type, we only realize how deeply capitalism is hurt by the Soviet Union. These attacks, friends and fellow-workers, are the surest sign that the Soviet Union is marching ahead, that it is bringing to larger and larger numbers of millions the message of liberation, that by its acts of freeing the Ukrainians, the Byelo-Russians, the Jews, brought about by its immensely increased strength, it is bringing in a new life, a new vision, a new hope into a world which the imperialists have thrust into an abyss of blood and tears.

The Soviets are marching on. The light of the Soviets is illuminating the world. The actions of the Soviets have opened new sunlit vistas before the eyes of mankind. Let the enemies rage. Freedom is marching on. National liberation is making new gains.

We greet the Soviet Union. I am quite confident I am speaking not only in my own name but in the name of millions of those belonging to national groups in the United States when I say:

Long live the Soviet Union, the liberator of oppressed nationalities!

* 9 7 8 1 4 7 0 1 2 7 0 0 8 *